D0753258

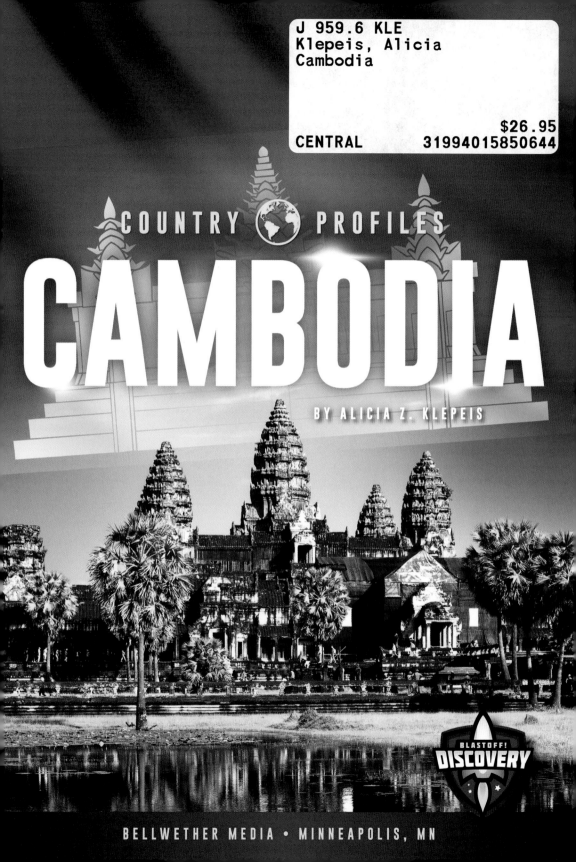

COUNTRY 🌐 PROFILES

# CAMBODIA

BY ALICIA Z. KLEPEIS

BLASTOFF!
DISCOVERY

BELLWETHER MEDIA • MINNEAPOLIS, MN

**Blastoff! Discovery** launches
a new mission: reading to learn.
Filled with facts and features, each
book offers you an exciting new
world to explore!

This edition first published in 2019 by Bellwether Media, Inc.

No part of this publication may be reproduced in whole or in part
without written permission of the publisher.
For information regarding permission, write to Bellwether Media, Inc.,
Attention: Permissions Department,
6012 Blue Circle Drive, Minnetonka, MN 55343.

Library of Congress Cataloging-in-Publication Data

Names: Klepeis, Alicia, 1971- author.
Title: Cambodia / by Alicia Z. Klepeis.
Description: Minneapolis, MN : Bellwether Media, Inc., 2019. |
    Series: Blastoff! Discovery. Country Profiles | Includes bibliographical
    references and index. | Audience: Grades 3-8.
Identifiers: LCCN 2018037201 (print) | LCCN 2018038047 (ebook)
    | ISBN 9781681036779 (ebook) | ISBN 9781626179592 |
    (hardcover : alk. paper)
Subjects:  LCSH: Cambodia–Juvenile literature.
Classification: LCC DS554.3 (ebook) | LCC DS554.3 .K55 2019
    (print) | DDC 959.6–dc23
LC record available at https://lccn.loc.gov/2018037201

Editor: Rebecca Sabelko    Designer: Brittany McIntosh

Printed in the United States of America, North Mankato, MN.

# TABLE OF CONTENTS

ANGKOR WAT

The sun rises over Siem Reap as a group of **tourists** prepares for their journey to Angkor Wat. Soon, they are amazed by the largest religious monument on Earth! This city of temples was built during the 12th century in honor of the Hindu god, Vishnu.

OTHER TOP SITES

PHNOM KAMPONG TRACH CAVE

ROYAL PALACE

SILVER PAGODA

TONLÉ SAP LAKE

The visitors study the beautiful stone carvings covering the temples. The carvings display gods, lions, and much more! The sun sparkles off the water in the **moat** surrounding Angkor Wat while a breeze rustles the palm trees. The sound of gibbons fills the air as the visitors explore the five central towers. Before leaving, they enjoy a picnic as the sun sets. Welcome to Cambodia!

N
W ➕ E
S

Cambodia is located in Southeast Asia and stretches across 69,898 square miles (181,035 square kilometers). Cambodia's capital, Phnom Penh, lies in the south-central part of the country along the Mekong River.

Cambodia is hugged on three sides by its neighboring countries. The country of Vietnam stretches along Cambodia's southeastern and eastern edge. To the north are the nations of Laos and Thailand. Thailand also curves around Cambodia's western border. The **Gulf** of Thailand washes upon Cambodia's beautiful southwestern beaches.

THAILAND

LAOS

SIEM REAP

BATTAMBANG

MEKONG
RIVER

CAMBODIA

PHNOM PENH

VIETNAM

SIHANOUKVILLE

GULF OF
THAILAND

## PARADISE ISLANDS

More than 60 islands lie off Cambodia's
southwestern coast. Their dense forests
and surrounding deep blue waters are
popular with tourists.

# LANDSCAPE AND CLIMATE

Cambodia is covered by a varied landscape. The center is a low-lying **plain**. Southeast Asia's largest lake, Tonlé Sap, lies within this plain. Thinly forested lowlands gradually rise into the Cardamom Mountains in the southwest and the Dângrêk Mountains in the north. Forested mountains and high

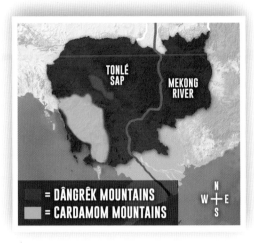

= DÂNGRÊK MOUNTAINS
= CARDAMOM MOUNTAINS

**plateaus** cover the eastern highlands. The Mekong, Cambodia's largest river, flows south into Vietnam before emptying into the South China Sea.

## UPS AND DOWNS

Tonlé Sap changes all year long. Parts of the lake might be just 3 feet (1 meter) deep in the dry season. But it can be 45 feet (14 meters) deep during the rainy season!

TONLÉ SAP

TATAI WATERFALL
KOH KONG

## PHNOM PENH

**Average seasonal highs and lows**

**JANUARY**
HIGH: 88 °F (31 °C)
LOW: 73 °F (23 °C)

**APRIL**
HIGH: 95 °F (35 °C)
LOW: 80 °F (27 °C)

**JULY**
HIGH: 90 °F (32 °C)
LOW: 79 °F (26 °C)

**OCTOBER**
HIGH: 87 °F (31 °C)
LOW: 78 °F (26 °C)

°F = degrees Fahrenheit
°C = degrees Celsius

Cambodia has a warm, **tropical** climate all year long. Seasonal winds called **monsoons** bring rain from May to October. The dry season from November to April is cooler and dry.

Cambodia is rich with wildlife! The Mekong River basin and other bodies of water are home to a variety of animals. Pelicans, ducks, and common kingfishers are among the many birds found there. Irrawaddy dolphins play in the current of the Mekong while Siamese crocodiles hunt for fish and other prey.

Clouded leopards and Asian elephants roam the **remote** forests in the eastern lowlands. Wild cattle called banteng make their home there, too. Sun bears, the smallest of any living bear **species**, rest on the forest floor, while deer watch from a distance.

IRRAWADDY DOLPHIN

SUN BEAR

KOUPREY

### HARD TO SPY

The kouprey is Cambodia's national mammal. Its name means "forest ox" in Khmer. Koupreys are very rare. One has not been seen in the wild since 1988.

COMMON KINGFISHER

SIAMESE
CROCODILE

# SIAMESE
# CROCODILE

Life Span: 25 years
Red List Status: critically endangered

Siamese crocodile range =

| LEAST CONCERN | NEAR THREATENED | VULNERABLE | ENDANGERED | CRITICALLY ENDANGERED | EXTINCT IN THE WILD | EXTINCT |
|---|---|---|---|---|---|---|
| | | | | ▲ | | |

More than 16 million people call Cambodia home. Most Cambodians belong to the Khmer **ethnic** group. The Khmer came to Cambodia from the north over a thousand years ago. The Cham are a **minority** group in Cambodia. They mainly live in villages along the Mekong and Tonlé Sap Rivers. Cambodia is also home to small groups of people from China and Vietnam.

Cambodia's official religion is Buddhism. Smaller groups of Cambodians practice other religions, including Islam and Christianity. Nearly everyone in Cambodia speaks Khmer, the nation's official language.

## FAMOUS FACE

Name: **Loung Ung**
Birthday: **April 17, 1970**
Hometown: **Phnom Penh, Cambodia**
Famous for: **Best-selling author and human rights activist who travels the world in support of human rights**

## SPEAK KHMER

**SIEM REAP**

Khmer uses script instead of letters. However, Khmer words can be written with the English alphabet so you can read them.

| ENGLISH | KHMER | HOW TO SAY IT |
|---|---|---|
| hello | susadei | soos-a-DAY |
| goodbye | lee hi | lee HI |
| please | som | sohm |
| thank you | arkun | ar-koon |
| yes (male) | bah | bah |
| yes (female) | jah | chaa |
| no | ot teh | ot tei |

# COMMUNITIES

Family is important to people in Cambodia. Many Cambodians live with extended family members. Grandparents, cousins, and aunts and uncles often live and work together. This is especially true in crowded cities like Siem Reap. There, many people live in apartments. They often travel by bus, bicycle, or motorbike.

SIEM REAP

TONLÉ SAP RIVER

About three out of every four people live in the Cambodian countryside. Many live in the areas near the Mekong and Tonlé Sap Rivers. **Rural** homes are often made of wood. Roofs can be **thatched** or made of clay tiles or metal. Many homes do not have electricity. But cell phone coverage is expanding in the countryside.

Cambodians greet each other with a gesture called the *sampeah*. This gesture involves pressing the hands together in a praying position in front of the chest. Holding the hands higher shows greater respect. Cambodians usually behave differently depending on who they are with. Often, people do not make eye contact with someone who is older or of a higher **status**.

Western-style clothing is common in Phnom Penh. But older Cambodians tend to dress more **traditionally**. Many wear *sarongs*, or large rectangular pieces of cloth that are wrapped around the waist.

## SHOWING RESPECT

Touching a person's head is very rude in Cambodia. In Buddhist culture, the head is holy.

*SARONG*

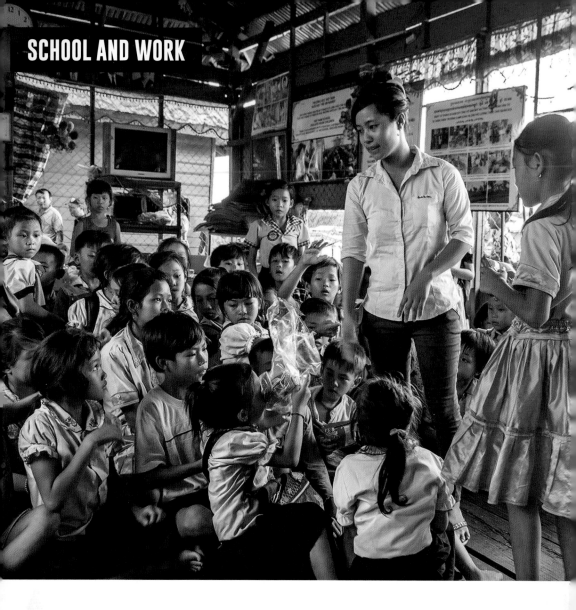

Students in Cambodia start school at age 6. Education from preschool to twelfth grade is free for many students. However, not all children finish school. Some families cannot afford to educate all of their children. Students who are able to complete secondary school can go on to study at universities or trade schools.

Nearly half of all Cambodians work in agriculture. Farmers grow rice, corn, vegetables, and **cassava**. Many others have **service jobs** in education, tourism, or health care. Other people **manufacture** products like clothing or footwear.

FABRIC MILL

RICE FARMER

19

BOKATOR

Soccer is Cambodia's most popular sport. Kids across the country play pick-up games. Sports fans love to watch the national team play. Some watch on TV. Others go to the huge stadium in Phnom Penh. Volleyball and *bokator*, a form of kickboxing, are other favorite sports throughout the country.

SOCCER

Many young people in Cambodia like to spend time with their friends. People in Phnom Penh often meet at restaurants or cafes or see live performances. It is also becoming popular to go to movie theaters and play video games.

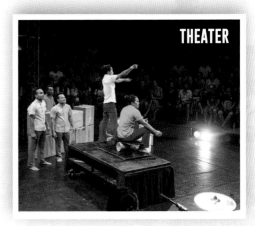

**THEATER**

# TRES

*Tres* is a popular game in Cambodia. People can play it alone or with a group. It is similar to jacks.

## What You Need:
- a lime or small ball
- 10 chopsticks or other thin sticks

## How to Play:
1. To begin, place the 10 chopsticks on a table.
2. Using only one hand, the first player tosses the lime in the air and tries to grab one chopstick before catching the lime.
3. The first player continues to toss the lime, grab one chopstick, and catch the lime until they make a mistake. A player makes a mistake when they do not catch the lime before grabbing a chopstick.
4. After a mistake, it is the other player's turn. The player who collects the most sticks wins!

## SPIDERY SNACKS

Fried tarantulas are a popular street food in Skuon. They may be served with rice or noodles. They are favorite snacks when cooked with garlic, sugar, and salt.

Most Cambodians start the day with *nom banh chok*, or Khmer noodles. This includes rice noodles with a fish gravy and fresh vegetables such as green beans and cucumbers. Dinner is the biggest meal of the day. People usually eat rice and soup. Sometimes, these are combined with vegetables or meat. Dishes like *loc lac*, a stir-fried beef with a sweet sauce, are common.

Some consider *fish amok* to be the country's national dish. The fish is cooked inside banana leaves with spices and coconut milk. Cambodians enjoy many tropical fruits like pineapple, mango, or *durian*, a spiky fruit with prickly skin.

LOC LAC

FISH AMOK

# BANANAS IN COCONUT MILK RECIPE

**Ingredients:**
4 large ripe bananas
1 cup thick coconut milk
1 tablespoon sugar

**Steps:**
1. Using the thick coconut milk at the top of the can, measure out one cup. Add some of the thinner liquid to make one full cup if necessary.

2. With the help of an adult, simmer the coconut milk and sugar in a saucepan until it is thick and creamy.

3. Peel the bananas, and cut each into three or four pieces.

4. Add the bananas to the coconut milk and sugar mixture. Cook over medium heat until the bananas are soft but not mushy. Serve warm!

# CELEBRATIONS

The Khmer New Year falls in mid-April in Cambodia. People celebrate the New Year for three days. They clean and decorate their homes. They also exchange gifts and help the poor. Cambodian Buddhists celebrate the birth of the **Buddha** in April or May. People offer food and other gifts to **monks**.

Cambodians celebrate their independence from France on November 9. Festivities across the country include parades and firework displays. The Royal Palace in Phnom Penh is lit up in the evening. Cambodians are excited to celebrate their nation and **culture** all year long!

KHMER NEW YEAR

ROYAL PALACE
DURING INDEPENDENCE DAY

**BEFORE 600 CE**
Trade with India and China influences culture and religions in Cambodia

**1975**
Pol Pot and the Khmer Rouge, a dangerous and violent political group, take control of Cambodia

**AROUND 1113**
Construction begins on Angkor Wat

**1941–1945**
Japan occupies Cambodia during World War II

**1863**
France begins its 90-year rule over Cambodia

## 1993
The first free and fair elections in decades take place

## 2001
The first bridge over the Mekong River opens, helping to boost trade in the region and encourage more tourists to visit Cambodia

## 1978-1979
Vietnamese invade Cambodia and overthrow the Khmer Rouge

## 2013
Construction begins on the Lower Sesan II Hydropower Dam, which aims to boost energy production in Cambodia

**Official Name:** Kingdom of Cambodia

**Flag of Cambodia:** Cambodia's flag has three horizontal bands of color. The top and bottom bands are blue. The central band is red. Both red and blue are traditional colors for Cambodia. In the middle of the flag is an outline of Angkor Wat.

**Area:** 69,898 square miles
(181,035 square kilometers)

**Capital City:** Phnom Penh

**Important Cities:** Siem Reap,
Battambang, Sihanoukville

**Population:**
16,204,486 (July 2017)

WHERE
PEOPLE LIVE

COUNTRYSIDE
**76.6%**

CITY
23.4%

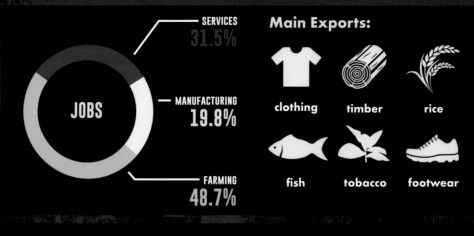

SERVICES
**31.5%**

**JOBS**

MANUFACTURING
**19.8%**

FARMING
**48.7%**

**Main Exports:**

clothing   timber   rice

fish   tobacco   footwear

**National Holiday:**
Independence Day (November 9)

**Main Language:**
Khmer

**Form of Government:**
parliamentary constitutional monarchy

**Title for Country Leaders:**
king (head of state)
prime minister (head of government)

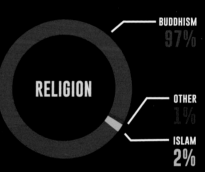

**RELIGION**

BUDDHISM
**97%**

OTHER
**1%**

ISLAM
**2%**

NATIONAL BANK OF CAMBODIA
2001

**Unit of Money:**
Cambodian riel

# GLOSSARY

**Buddha**—a man from India originally named Siddhartha Gautama; Buddha is the founder of Buddhism.

**cassava**—a tropical plant with starchy, edible roots

**culture**—the beliefs, arts, and ways of life in a place or society

**ethnic**—related to a group of people who share customs and an identity

**gulf**—part of an ocean or sea that extends into land

**manufacture**—to make products, often with machines

**minority**—a group of people fewer in number than another group

**moat**—a wide, deep trench around the walls of a large building or castle that is usually filled with water

**monks**—men who have given up all their belongings to become part of a specific religious community

**monsoons**—winds that shift direction each season; monsoons bring heavy rain.

**plain**—a large area of flat land

**plateaus**—areas of flat, raised land

**remote**—located far from large cities or populated areas

**rural**—related to the countryside

**service jobs**—jobs that perform tasks for people or businesses

**species**—a group of animals or plants that are similar and can produce young

**status**—position or rank in relation to others

**thatched**—having a roof covering made of grass or straw

**tourists**—people who travel to visit another place

**traditionally**—according to the customs, ideas, or beliefs handed down from one generation to the next

**tropical**—part of the tropics; the tropics is a hot, rainy region near the equator.

# TO LEARN MORE

## AT THE LIBRARY

Mara, Wil. *Cambodia*. New York, N.Y.: Children's Press, 2018.

Oachs, Emily Rose. *Vietnam*. Minneapolis, Minn.: Bellwether Media, 2018.

Sheehan, Sean, Barbara Cooke, and Caitlyn Miller. *Cambodia*. New York, N.Y.: Cavendish Square, 2017.

## ON THE WEB

**FACTSURFER**

Factsurfer.com gives you a safe, fun way to find more information.

1. Go to www.factsurfer.com.

2. Enter "Cambodia" into the search box.

3. Click the "Surf" button and select your book cover to see a list of related web sites.

# INDEX